Echoes of September 11

Alex Telman

Published by Alex Telman, 2024.

ECHOES OF SEPTEMBER 11

First edition. September 11, 2024.

ISBN: 979-8230674290

Written by Alex Telman.

Table of Contents

DEDICATIONS

To Those Who Lost Their Lives

In morning's light, the towers fell so fast,
Their shadows long, now etched in time's own grace.
Each name a star, a memory to last,
In hearts where echoes find their sacred place.
For every life that passed, we hold you dear,
Your light remains, though you are no longer near.

To Those Frontline Workers And Others Who Risked Their Lives

Brave souls who stood where danger roared its might,
You ventured forth where others feared to tread.
In smoky haze and chaos of the sight,
Your courage shone as you to darkness wed.
With every step, your hero's heart displayed,
A beacon bright through shadows' grim parade.

To Those Who Survived and Have Been Permanently Affected

From rubble's edge, you rise to greet each day,
Though scars remain, your spirit bears the strain.
In lives transformed, your strength lights up the way,
A testament to overcoming pain.
For every trial, your resilience blooms,
In shadows cast, your hopeful spirit looms.

To the Relatives of Those Affected and Their Traumas

In grief's embrace, you've carried heavy hearts,
Through endless nights and days of aching thought.
The pain of loss, where memory never parts,
In silent tears and solace dearly sought.
To those who mourn and bear the endless weight,
Your love endures, though time may hesitate.

To Future Generations – May They Learn Lessons

May wisdom from the past guide paths ahead,
And lessons learned from sorrow's deep embrace.
In every tale of loss, let hope be spread,
To shape a world where peace and love find place.
For future hearts, may understanding grow,
From shadows past, let brighter futures glow.

Author's Note

Writing about the September 11 attacks, even now, years later, is a process that demands deep reflection and emotional honesty. It is impossible to separate that day from the visceral experiences so many of us had—whether we were watching the events unfold in real time, hearing the news through loved ones, or feeling the collective grief settle across the world. Time has a way of muting certain aspects of trauma, but it never fully erases the emotional landscape carved by such moments. In these poems, I wanted to explore not just the immediate reactions to the attack, but the slow evolution of grief and resilience that followed, both individually and as a society.

When something as catastrophic as the fall of the Twin Towers happens, we often focus first on the shock, the devastation, and the immediate response—the smoke, the dust, the confusion. But it is in the days, months, and years that follow where we begin to understand how profoundly such an event has altered us. The first poem captures that immediate aftermath: the stunned disbelief, the weight of silence after the towers fell, the desperate attempts to process something that, at the time, seemed too enormous to comprehend. It speaks to the fragility we suddenly became aware of, how easily our sense of security and normalcy could be shattered.

The second poem, written as if standing in the wreckage a month later, reflects a world still holding its breath. By this time, the initial shock has subsided, but the grief remains, heavy and constant. I wanted to convey that sense of weight- the way loss lingers even after the smoke has cleared, how life tries to move forward but is forever marked by what was lost. We begin to memorialize, to create spaces where we can gather and remember, and yet we carry the knowledge that memory itself cannot rebuild what is gone. The city, like its people, starts to adjust, but there is no returning to the world as it once was.

One year later, as reflected in the third poem, there is a quiet, almost reluctant acceptance of the new reality. We have become accustomed to the absence in the skyline, the gap in our collective lives. Grief no longer roars but hums in the background, a permanent undercurrent to our days. The memorials grow, the names etched in stone, but there is a palpable shift from raw pain to endurance. Time has passed, and we are still here, though changed. The world feels different, and though we have found ways to move forward, we still carry the scars, both visible and unseen.

Perhaps the most profound change, however, is not in the skyline or in the physical remnants of the attack, but in the hearts and minds of those who lived through it. The question, "How did we change?" is not easily answered, because it encompasses so much. We became more aware of our vulnerability, realizing that even in a world of towering achievements, we are not immune to devastation. We became more cautious, more vigilant, and in many ways, more fearful. But at the same time, we also learned to cherish the small, ordinary moments that once went unnoticed—the way the sun still rises, the way people still find joy, even in the aftermath of unimaginable loss.

These poems are not just about mourning; they are also about resilience. They speak to the human ability to survive, even in the face of such profound tragedy. We rebuild, not because we have forgotten, but because we must. We carry forward the memory of what was lost, but we do not let it define us entirely. The attacks changed us, yes, but they also revealed a depth of strength and compassion that we might not have known we possessed. In the face of destruction, we learned to hold each other closer, to build new things- relationships, communities, even skylines- that would endure.

In writing these poems, I was struck by how grief evolves. It is not static; it shifts and changes with time, sometimes retreating to the background, only to surge forward unexpectedly. In the immediate aftermath, we are often too numb to fully understand the magnitude of our loss. It is only later, as we try to return to our routines, that the weight of it settles in. These poems reflect that process, the slow, difficult work of integrating tragedy into the fabric of our lives without letting it define us entirely. They are about the passage of time and the way memory becomes a kind of architecture in itself—a way of holding what was lost while still making room for what remains.

Ultimately, these reflections are not just about a single event, but about the universal experience of loss and survival. The attacks on September 11 left an indelible mark on the world, but they also illuminated the ways in which we, as human beings, adapt and endure. In the face of horror, we build memorials- not just physical ones, but emotional ones, too. We honor the lives lost by living our own lives more fully, by refusing to let the darkness overshadow the light that remains.

These poems are an attempt to give voice to that process, to reflect on the ways we have changed and the ways we have stayed the same. They are about memory, loss, and resilience, but most of all, they are about what it means to be human in the face of unimaginable grief. We carry on, not because we forget, but because remembering is part of what it means to live.

Alex

Introduction

In the early hours of September 11, 2001, the world witnessed a profound tragedy that would forever alter the course of history. As the Twin Towers crumbled and the skyline of New York City was forever changed, a collective sense of grief and bewilderment enveloped us all. The events of that fateful day not only challenged our understanding of security and resilience but also laid bare the complexities of human emotion and memory.

This collection of poems, born from the ashes of that day, seeks to capture the multifaceted experiences and reflections surrounding the September 11 attacks. Each poem is a fragment of a larger narrative- a testament to the lives lost, the heroes who risked everything, the survivors who continue to bear the weight of their trauma, and the families whose lives were irrevocably altered. Through these verses, we honor their stories and explore the profound impact of this historical moment.

Purpose and Inspiration

The inspiration for these poems stems from a deep-seated need to process and understand the immense sorrow and resilience that emerged from September 11. Writing these poems has been an act of reflection and homage- a way to give voice to the silent echoes of that day and to offer a canvas for the raw emotions that linger in its wake. Each poem serves as a lens through which we examine not just the immediate aftermath but also the ongoing journey of healing and remembrance.

Impact on Readers

The intended impact of this book is twofold: to offer a space for contemplation and to inspire hope. As readers delve into these poems, they will encounter a tapestry of emotions- grief, courage, and hope- woven together to reflect the complexity of human experience. The poems are designed to evoke a deep emotional response and encourage readers to engage with the themes of loss, recovery, and renewal.

In honoring the memory of those who perished, celebrating the bravery of those who served, and acknowledging the enduring pain of survivors and their families, this book aims to foster a greater understanding of the human spirit's capacity for resilience. It is a reminder that, even in the face of profound adversity, there is a possibility for growth, healing, and hope.

Looking Forward

As we turn the pages of this book, let us remember that the journey from tragedy to healing is not a linear path but a mosaic of shared experiences and collective strength. The poems contained within are a tribute to the past, a reflection on the present, and a beacon for the future. May they serve as a reminder of our shared humanity and the enduring power of hope in the face of unimaginable challenges.

In the end, this collection is not just a recounting of events but a call to honor the lessons learned and to carry forward the spirit of resilience and compassion. It is my hope that these poems will resonate deeply with you and inspire a continued commitment to understanding, empathy, and renewal.

The Twin Towers of Love

Words on a page are irreversible, invincible,
they bury our senses then magnify our sorrows-
twenty six letters are all I have
to make sense of this pain
and fill the canyon between my heart and your head.
Words on a page cannot heal
when mankind's meanings change-
when meanings change
the journey needs to be redefined,
and old words, and old meanings, have no meaning.
When words are in shock, worlds collapse.
Better to write than do nothing? No!
Better to write than do nothing?
No, better to listen to the silence, and
we all deserve a moment of silence,
shhhhhhhhhh...
Say nothing. Do nothing. Be still.
Can you hear it -
the whimpering whispers
of falling angels
wrapped in dust,
not angel dust,
but the hot grey ash
of a crumbling civilisation.
In one mad moment

ALEX TELMAN

those planes licked the windows
of our civilisation
and our sense of security
panicked and jumped out of that window,
and fell...
and the world breathed pain
and fear melted our infrastructure
and I asked,
"what use is poetry?
what use is theatre?
what use is music?
what use is art?
what use is fiction?
what use is reality?"
gone Ginsberg,
gone Burroughs
gone Bukowski,
gone William Carlos Williams,
gone Lennon,
gone Hendrix,
gone Joplin,
gone Martin Luther King,
gone JF Kennedy,
gone Malcolm X.....
gone gone gone, gone gone gone gone gone,
gone gone gone gone gone gone gone gone
Someone tried to light a candle
but tears kept putting it out
and a child asked, "Did God die today?"
and you asked, "Did love die today?"
and I asked, "Does it matter,
if you don't lay next me no more?"

ECHOES OF SEPTEMBER 11

You are gone,
extinguished from my life.
I am one dark speck
in a constellation crushed by celestial ash,
like a delicate wave
consumed by its own froth,
like some ancient stain
fossilised into frozen desire,
submerged by the torment
of moment by moment eternities,
sitting on my balcony
waiting for the phone to ring.
It doesn't.
You are gone.
No more
you and I will merge,
sealed by a relentless tenderness
as it collapses suddenly
into a suffocating
torrent of ash.
You were the valley
of a single petal,
now burnt to nothingness.
Under your skin
the world came alive
and time had no Time
and words needed no Words,
and the twin landscapes of your eyes
will embed you in my verse forever
and my finger trembling down your spine
will always in my mind
split the loveliness of your back

into
two
towers
of
love,
until, after one final moment of loving tenderness,
the freshness of our primal touch collapsed...
I loved you without knowing why,
I loved you without knowing how,
I loved you without knowing doubt,
but the demon in you,
the hermit,
the recluse
extinguished our flame into a nothingness
that words could not stop,
that words could not stop.
Now we all live on Ground Zero,
we all live alone;
we are an endangered species,
we are reason on a broken skyline, and
the day weighs heavy on the sidewalks
of an ashen hell,
and mankind was bitten by the demons of one man,
a hermit,
a recluse-
injecting the world with a toxic nightmare
that words could stop, that words cannot stop.
Stop running from the truth
stop running from each other
stop running from your self,
and stop this military solution
to all your inner problems.

ECHOES OF SEPTEMBER 11

Look through your pupils of fire,
look through you eyelids of ash;
we all breathed the dead with ash in our eyes
and it forced me to deny the supremacy of our architecture,
and it forced me to deny the supremacy of our technology,
and it forced me to deny the supremacy of our military,
and it forced me to deny the supremacy of our government,
and it forced me to deny the supremacy of capitalism,
and it forced me to deny the supremacy of our leadership,
and it forced me to deny the supremacy of our nationhood,
and it forced me to deny the supremacy of Christianity,
and it forced me to deny the supremacy of Islam,
and it forced me to deny the supremacy of Judaism,
and it forced me to deny the supremacy of Buddhism,
and it forced me to deny the supremacy of ego...
the supremacy of ego-
- the supremacy of ego
is what got us into this mess
in the first place!
This place,
standing on the 100th floor
of a crippled civilisation:
a civilisation built on anger
a civilisation built on greed
a civilisation built on lust
a civilisation built on ego
a civilisation built on captions-
Ground Zero is a caption,
a marketing ploy,
sexy today, forgotten tomorrow-
Did the Coliseum have a one hundredth floor?
Did the Pyramids have a one hundredth floor?

ALEX TELMAN

Did the Hippodrome have a one hundredth floor?
Did the Haghia Sophia have a one hundredth floor?
Did the Liurong Temple have a one hundredth floor?
Did the Temple of Solomon have a one hundredth floor?
Are these smouldering in a heap of smoking memory?
Words on a page
cannot undo the pain
cannot undo the torment
cannot undo the affliction
These are irreversible,
irreversible;
we as a species are
irreversible.
We thought we were adults,
only to realise we are infants bathing in putrid waters.
We as a civilisation thought we were indestructible,
only to find ourselves smouldering
in a heap of smoking memory.
One sting of bitter wretchedness,
one strain of inflamed torment
ripped the heart out of every pen
held in the frightened fingers
of every poet,
and delivered a cry that shattered every city,
butchering the Universal Soul
that had taken 10,000 years to cement
into some tenuous semblance of civilisation,
... semblance of civilisation.
We are alive
at a time after death,
and after death we pick up the pieces
of angels beaten by Time-

ECHOES OF SEPTEMBER 11

the broken pottery of consciousness,
the burnt paper of creativity,
the speechless mouthing of a language dying of shock:
"Oh my God!"
"This can't be happening!"
"Unreal!"
"Get outta here!"
"Go figure!"
"No way, man!"
and the answer is not blowing in the wind-
it never was-
it's in the heart and mind of one mad person
who chose not to leave us alone.
And our answer lies is stillness,
in silence,
in being left alone,
in silence,
shhhhhhhhhhh...
Say nothing.
Do nothing.
Be still.
Can you hear it -
the whimpering whispers
of falling angels
wrapped in dust,
not angel dust,
but the hot grey ash
of a crumbling civilisation.
We all deserve a moment of silence.
I never read the papers
and now I understand why-
Where is the happiness in history

ALEX TELMAN

Where is the playfulness in history?
Where is the light-heartedness in history?
Where is the contentment?
History is a series of labels
and labels are throw-away lies,
disposable truths,
and our civilisation is built on disposable truths,
and whether we like it or not we are caught
between the disposable and the dispensable.
Nothing in this poem is original,
nor is it meant to be.
Originality died 3,000 deaths ago.
Words could not get you back-
they are air.
Words can not replace our civilisation-
it is air.
Words on a page are irreversible.
History as labels is disposable
and all we are left with are words-
history is a junkyard of words...
poetry is a junkyard of words...
and our answer still lies in stillness,
in silence,
in being left alone,
in silence,
shhhhhhhhhh...
Say nothing.
Do nothing.
Be still.
Can you hear it -
the whimpering whispers
of falling angels

ECHOES OF SEPTEMBER 11

wrapped in dust,
not angel dust,
but the hot grey ash
of a crumbling civilisation...
We all deserve a moment of silence.
Sept 15, 2001

The Screen Flickers as the Towers Burn

I.

It began as a morning like any other.
Coffee cooling in my hands,
the clatter of the world on television-
but there was something strange in the air,
a pause between sentences,
as if the anchor herself had forgotten how to breathe.
And then, the picture shifted-
the city I knew,
but not the city I knew.
Smoke curling from the tower,
a wound in the sky.
I blinked, expecting the scene to rearrange,
to make sense in a way it didn't.
But it stayed-
this new geometry of fear,
this sharp, jagged line across the skyline
where life had broken open.
What was this?
A dream perhaps,
or some fiction playing across the screen,
the way they show explosions in films,
neat, controlled,
and unreal.
But this-

this was no film.
The fire climbed higher,
consuming everything in its path,
and the silence in the room pressed hard against my chest.

II.

I could feel it-
the world shifting beneath me,
though I sat perfectly still.
The coffee went cold,
forgotten.
I stared into the smoke,
into the terror
that leapt from the screen to my living room,
as though I could step into it
and touch the flames myself.
People moved in the distance-
too small to see clearly,
but they ran,
ran like something was chasing them,
though there was no escape,
only the dust and the dark.
The camera trembled-
or maybe it was me-
as the second plane came,
a thing of steel and fury,
silent until the impact ripped the sky open.
It hit like a punch to the gut,
and suddenly I was no longer watching-
I was there,
in the thick of it,
my heart pounding

like the beat of a thousand unanswered prayers.

III.

I could hear the cries,
though no sound came through the screen.
The faces, pixelated and frozen,
blurred between the smoke and the falling glass.
They were jumping now-
one after another,
leaping into the void
as if they might fly.
I wanted to look away,
but I couldn't.
My eyes were trapped,
locked to the image of bodies in freefall,
the slow descent,
their final embrace with gravity.
How do you hold onto hope
when there is nothing to hold onto
but air?
The world felt like it was ending.
I think I said it aloud-
the words hanging in the room like vapor,
waiting for someone to respond,
but there was only the television,
its endless reel of destruction.

IV.

Minutes passed, or maybe hours.
Time had no meaning in that moment.
It stretched and folded in on itself,
just like the towers collapsing in slow motion-

a wave of dust and ruin,
swallowing everything below.
The screen turned gray,
the city erased
by its own bones.
What do we do now?
I thought,
but the thought felt too small,
too simple for what was happening.
There were no answers.
There was only the smoke
that spiraled into the sky,
taking with it whatever certainties
we had once believed.
And yet,
the news went on,
its cycle of horror
repeating,
showing the same images,
as if we hadn't yet learned to believe them.

V.

I reached for the phone,
my fingers trembling,
unsure of who to call
or what to say.
The words felt too fragile-
how do you say, "Are you safe?"
when safety itself has fallen
like the towers?
How do you breathe
when the air is thick with fear,

ALEX TELMAN

when the world,
your world,
is crumbling before your eyes?
I didn't know.
I only knew that nothing would be the same-
the towers would not rise again,
and neither would we.
There were voices on the television,
but I had stopped listening.
What could they say
that would matter now?
All that remained was the silence-
the silence behind the screams,
the silence that stretched between the moments
of the towers' fall.
I sat there,
watching the dust
and the smoke
and the hollow sky,
waiting for something-
though I knew not what.
Only that it would never come.
Written a few Hours after the Attack September 11, 2001

The Day After

I.

The streets are filled with broken shadows,
gray like ash from a forgotten fire.
Between the cracks of silence, echoes rise-
not voices, but something hollow, deeper still-
the hum of absence.
Across the river, the skyline stands amputated,
an empty mouth gasping for air.
The eyes of the city turn upward,
searching, but there is nothing-
only a scattering of ghosts,
dust circling in a windless void.
The towers were stories
stacked upon stories,
now collapsed into rubble,
a memory fragmented by gravity.
Who will gather these fragments?
Who will build a song from the smoke?
The wind carries the weight of lost names,
but there is no temple here,
no ground for lamentation.

II.

In the cafe, the news drones on,
a static recitation of broken lives.

We listen without listening,
our hearts folded inward,
our hands, idle as abandoned prayer books.
Each face in the mirror looks unfamiliar today,
the lines deeper, etched by something nameless,
a grief that hides behind glass.
The city murmurs beneath its skin-
subways creak like bones,
the river sighs under its bridges-
but it is the silence we hear most clearly now,
a silence that fills our lungs with the weight of iron.
Who counts the cost of such silence?
What is lost when towers fall but time remains,
trapped in the moments before the end?

III.

There are no more words for this,
only symbols:
a shoe in the dust,
a briefcase spilled on the corner,
papers that rise like leaves in September winds,
carrying a message no one will read.
Who will decipher this language of collapse?
The architecture of grief is not made of brick or steel,
but of forgotten breaths, unfinished thoughts-
the last thing someone said before the world fell quiet.
We are architects of loss,
building shrines out of smoke,
hoping to trap the moment when it all changed,
but time slides past us, indifferent,
a river that refuses to bend.

IV.

And still, the morning comes-
a pale light over the Hudson,
a sun that seems too cruel, too bright
for this world of shattered glass and steel.
Who has the right to speak of hope
when the ground beneath us is shifting sand?
Yet, still we speak,
still we rise to face the day.
On this island of dreams,
built on bones and ambition,
we stand,
grieving,
waiting for the dust to settle.
But the dust does not settle.
It hangs in the air,
a silent witness,
a question without answer,
and the city, though broken,
does not sleep.
Written September 12/13, 2001

One Month Later

One Month Later: reflections on the process of moving forward, while still feeling the weight of what happened, a month after the attack. It captures the subtle, persistent grief and the new reality that people must navigate.

I.

The smoke has cleared,
but the air still feels heavy,
as if the weight of what's been lost
clings to every breath.
A month has passed,
and yet it feels both distant and near-
the towers still falling
in the back of our minds,
crumbling again with each new silence.
We walk the same streets
but nothing is the same.
The city hums beneath its skin,
nervous and watchful,
each footstep an echo of what came before,
as if waiting for something
that has already happened.

II.

Memorials bloom like flowers

where the dust once rose,
candles flicker in the evening winds,
their light small but stubborn
against the darkness we now carry.
What is this grief
that settles in like an old tenant?
It is no longer raw,
but quiet,
steady,
a rhythm we have learned to live with-
the ache that hums behind the noise
of moving forward.
We wear it like a second skin,
this grief,
as if by carrying it
we can somehow hold onto what was lost.

III.

The world still spins,
but it feels different-
the axis shifted just slightly,
enough that we sense the tilt
though we can't quite name it.
We are learning a new vocabulary-
"before" and "after"
now cleaved by a single day,
a line drawn in smoke
across the skyline.
Before, we knew how to live,
how to trust the ground beneath us.
After, we tread lightly,
unsure of what lies ahead,

only that it won't be what it was.

IV.

The calendar turns,
but the clock does not move.
It is always September in our hearts,
always that blue sky split open,
the perfect day ruined by flame and fall.
And we,
standing on the edges of time,
gathering the pieces
of something we can never rebuild.
There are still gaps in the skyline,
but larger ones in our lives-
names we no longer speak,
faces we only see in dreams.
We hold them close,
as if memory itself could keep them here.

V.

One month later,
and we are still trying to make sense
of the senseless.
We sift through the debris
of our own emotions,
picking out what we can carry,
leaving the rest to the wind.
There is no grand conclusion here,
no resolution.
Only the slow march of days
and the quiet resolve
to remember.

ECHOES OF SEPTEMBER 11

Not just the loss,
but the lives that were lived
in the shadow of the towers-
each one a story
that deserved more time.
And so we move forward,
but not past-
for the past is still here,
woven into the fabric of now,
a scar we will bear
long after the dust has settled.
Written October 13, 2001

One Year Later

One Year Later is a reflective poem that captures the emotions and the evolving perspective on the one-year anniversary of the attacks, a time when the shock has worn away, but the grief and memories remain deeply embedded.

I.

One year,
and the calendar returns to the day
we can never forget.
September hangs heavy in the air,
a weight that drags through every hour.
The city stands,
but something is missing-
a gap,
an absence that speaks louder
than any monument could.
We have learned to live around the loss,
but not past it.
The wound has scabbed over,
but it still aches
when the wind blows
just the wrong way.
The skyline is whole,
and yet broken,

a scar that the eye can't avoid.

II.

There is silence now where once there was smoke.
But silence, too, is heavy-
a reminder of what was here,
and what can never be rebuilt.
The towers were made of steel and glass,
but their fall left ghosts
woven into the bricks of this city,
into the bones of those who remain.
We live among them.
We walk past the space they filled,
feeling the echo,
the hollow where they once stood
like sentinels of the sky.
And though we move forward,
it is with eyes that never quite stop glancing back.

III.

What does it mean to heal
when the loss is too vast for words?
We have built shrines out of memory-
names carved in stone,
flowers laid at the base of the absent towers.
But healing is a quiet thing,
a slow, reluctant opening of the heart
to the world as it now is,
to the scar that shapes us.
We have rebuilt-
but not in the way we once imagined.
Not in steel or glass,

but in the stories we tell,
in the hands we reach for in the dark.
The skyline is not the same,
but neither are we.

IV.

And yet, time moves.
A year has passed,
the seasons turned over,
and still, the world spins.
We mark the day,
but life hums on,
in small, insistent ways-
the birth of a child,
the bloom of a flower in the park,
the laughter that finds us,
despite everything.
Grief has folded itself
into the rhythm of our days.
It does not ask for permission anymore;
it simply stays,
a quiet companion,
a reminder of what was lost
and what we carry forward.

V.

One year later,
and we are still here-
bearing the weight of memory,
but also the resilience
that comes from surviving.
The city breathes again,

though its lungs are forever changed.
The streets, though scarred,
still pulse with life.
We remember,
but we do more than remember.
We live.
We build again-
not to replace what was taken,
but to honor it,
to say:
this is what remains.
This is what endures.
And so, we stand,
beneath the same blue sky,
not untouched by grief,
but still reaching,
still rising,
still here.
Written September 11, 2002

The Lessons We've Learned

We stood in a world divided by smoke,
The sky, once endless, severed in its flight,
As towers crumbled, hearts in silence broke,
A single morning gave birth to the night.
The echo of our fragility rang,
Each breath we drew, a testament to fear,
Yet, through the ruin, voices softly sang,
Reminding us that hope still lingers near.
The first lesson we learned in the debris
Was that our strength is woven in unity.
We learned how swiftly peace could be undone,
How monuments of steel could turn to dust,
And in the burning shadow of the sun,
We held our neighbor's hand, because we must.
The strength we found was forged through shared despair,
In unity, we learned to rise from prayer.
We found in strangers what we'd lost in stone-
The comfort of knowing we're not alone.
For every person lost, a thousand hearts
Beat with the memory that love imparts.
Through shattered glass and smoke-filled skies, we grew,
Learning that, in the end, love pulls us through.
Years passed, the skyline gaped, a hollow frame,
Yet grief grew quieter, a softer hum-
The city, though reborn, was not the same,

For time had changed the face of everyone.
The ache that followed us, it never healed,
But hardened into something like resolve.
Though wounds ran deep, a brighter truth revealed
That we, through loss, would learn how to evolve.
We learned the weight of each ordinary day,
That safety, once assumed, can slip away.
The mundane became sacred: the morning's light,
The sound of laughter, the quiet of night.
The smallest things we took for granted, grew
Into reminders of what's brave and true.
We saw that life was delicate as glass,
Its beauty etched in fleeting, fragile strands,
And cherished every moment as it passed,
More aware of time's weight in our hands.
In tears, we built what hatred sought to rend-
A future, shaped by love, that would transcend.
Though fear had knocked upon our open door,
We learned that courage often comes from more-
From grief, from love, from hands that lift and guide,
And from the silent strength that lives inside.
From ashes rose the knowledge of our strength,
That suffering, though cruel, does not define,
And while the road to healing stretched in length,
We walked together, tethered by a line-
A bond that, even through the darkest days,
Refused to falter, crumble, or decay.
We learned to rebuild in a thousand ways,
To carve our sorrows into hope and clay.
From memory we crafted something new,
A bridge to carry us from grief to view
The world not through the lens of fear and hate,

But with a heart renewed, a clearer state.
The lesson here, in fire and smoke engraved,
Is not of vengeance, nor of burning rage,
But of a quiet courage deeply saved,
A wisdom earned through every mournful stage.
For though destruction knocked us to the ground,
In love and grace, our truest strength is found.
We learned compassion's quiet, steady hand
Could guide us through what we don't understand.
In pain, we chose connection, not the sword,
To build a peace that fear could not afford.
The towers fell, but in their place we grew-
Not just in steel and glass, but in our hearts,
For every tear, a kindness overdue,
For every scar, the will to make new starts.
And in the space between those silent streets,
Where dust and memory swirl in the breeze,
We learned that even brokenness completes,
That loss can forge a deeper peace with ease.
What hatred hoped to fracture, we embraced-
Our shared humanity could not be erased.
Each year, each name, each stone upon the ground,
Reminds us of the strength that we have found.
We've learned that time, though cruel, can also heal,
That in the cracks of tragedy, there's light,
And while the pain remains a thing we feel,
We move forward, with purpose and with might.
For even in the shadows cast by loss,
We've learned to lift each other, bear the cross.
The strength of nations lies not in their walls,
But in the way they rise when darkness falls.
We carry on, not just because we should-

But because, in the end, we know we could.
Let this be the story of our survival,
A testament to the human soul's revival,
For in the ashes of that fateful hour,
We learned to find resilience, hope, and power.
The past may haunt, but it will not confine-
In grief, we learn to build, to love, to shine.
We gather in the name of all we've lost,
And though the winds of time have left us tossed,
We rise, because our spirit will endure,
Stronger, wiser, braver, and more pure.
These lessons, born in smoke and endless flame,
Now guide us forward, different, yet the same.
We stand as witness to the strength we've earned-
This is the greatest lesson we have learned.

How Do We Heal?

Healing after a profound tragedy, like September 11, is a complex and deeply personal journey. It involves both individual and collective efforts to reconcile with the past while finding ways to move forward. Healing does not mean forgetting, but learning to carry the weight of loss in a way that allows us to live fully again. Here's how we begin to heal:

Acknowledge the Pain

Healing begins with acknowledging the depth of the pain. We must give space to the grief, anger, and confusion that comes with loss. Ignoring or suppressing these emotions only prolongs the healing process. To heal, we must first be honest about the scars we bear and the impact that loss has had on our lives.

Honor the Memories

Part of healing is learning how to remember. Creating memorials, holding anniversaries, and telling the stories of those we lost are ways of honoring their lives. These acts of remembrance help us hold onto their legacy without being consumed by the sorrow. We heal by finding ways to celebrate their lives and keeping their memory alive.

Lean on Each Other

Healing is not something we do alone. We heal as a community, leaning on the support of friends, family, and neighbors. Shared experiences create a bond that can lift us up when the weight of grief feels too heavy. In the aftermath of a tragedy, we learn that healing comes from connection, from the act of being there for one another, offering comfort, and receiving it in turn.

Find Meaning in the Loss

It's difficult to make sense of tragedy, but part of healing is finding meaning in the aftermath. We often ask "Why?"-why did this happen, why did we lose so much? While answers may be elusive, we can seek meaning by looking at how loss has shaped us, what lessons we've learned, and how we've grown in response. Healing can come when we find purpose in how we choose to live after the loss.

Rebuild with Purpose

After destruction comes the act of rebuilding- not just physically, but emotionally. This is a crucial step in healing. Rebuilding signifies hope, a declaration that life will continue. It also offers us the chance to create something new. We can rebuild stronger, more intentionally, with the lessons we've learned guiding us forward. Healing comes through the act of creation, through planting seeds of hope in the soil of loss.

Allow Time to Do Its Work

Healing is not something that happens overnight. It's a gradual process that unfolds with time. As time passes, the sharpness of the pain dulls, and the grief becomes part of who we are, a companion that walks beside us, not in front of us. We learn to live with loss, to integrate it into our lives without letting it consume us. Time doesn't erase the past, but it helps us soften our relationship with it, allowing healing to take root.

Embrace Resilience and Hope

Finally, healing requires hope. It requires us to believe that even in the face of profound loss, there is still beauty, still life, still a future worth living. Healing is about resilience- about bouncing back from the brink, finding light in the darkness, and learning to live fully again. It's a quiet strength that whispers, "We will endure."

Ultimately, we heal by continuing to live. We heal by embracing the small moments of joy, by building new relationships, and by refusing to let grief define our future. Healing is not about forgetting what happened—it's about learning to carry the memory of it with grace and finding ways to move forward with love, hope, and resilience in our hearts.

Reflections

In the moments after the sky split open and the towers fell, the world paused. We watched as steel turned to dust, as the unthinkable unfolded before our eyes. There were no words for the silence that followed. Only the thud of hearts breaking in unison, a collective gasp that echoed across oceans. The air was thick with grief, a weight so tangible it pressed into the very fabric of our lives. We held onto each other because there was nothing else to hold onto, nothing else that made sense in a world that had suddenly been torn asunder. There were no answers then, just the raw, incomprehensible truth of our vulnerability. We learned that day how fragile we were, how quickly the world could shift from mundane to catastrophic. But in the rubble of our disbelief, something stirred.

At first, it was quiet, barely perceptible amid the cries of anguish. But it grew, this realization: that even in the face of such destruction, we were not alone. People reached out across the chasm of loss, hands outstretched in a gesture older than language. We saw it in the way strangers became neighbors, in the way cities embraced those left stranded, in the way the world, for a moment, stood still in solidarity. We learned that unity was not just a word, but a force—one that could bind us together even as the ground beneath us crumbled. We learned the power of compassion, of connection, of standing shoulder to shoulder in the face of unimaginable pain.

There were tears, yes- rivers of them, flowing endlessly for the lives lost, for the innocence shattered, for the certainty we thought we possessed. But there was also resolve. There, amidst the smoke and ash, we made a vow, silent but sacred: we would rebuild. Not just the buildings, not just the skyline. We would rebuild ourselves. We would find a way to carry the weight of this tragedy without letting it define us, without letting it crush us. In the quiet of the days that followed, as we sifted through the remnants of what had been, we discovered a resilience we didn't know we had. A resilience born not from steel or stone, but from the human spirit's capacity to endure, to rise again.

The lessons came slowly, like dawn breaking after a long, dark night. We learned that fear could be confronted, that grief could be transformed into action. We learned to cherish the ordinary, the mundane- the things we once overlooked. A cup of coffee in the morning, the sound of children laughing, the comfort of a familiar routine. These became the threads we wove into our days, reminders that life, though fragile, was still here, still worth living, still filled with moments of grace. We learned that in the wake of devastation, love persists. It lingers in the air, in the spaces between, in the hands that rebuild what was broken.

But we also learned that scars do not fade easily. The pain of that day is still with us, woven into the fabric of our collective memory. It is a part of who we are now, part of the story we carry forward. And yet, those scars remind us of something vital: we survived. We survived because we chose to face the darkness, not with hatred or vengeance, but with hope. We learned that in the face of violence, the most radical act is to live fully, to love deeply, to hold onto the things that cannot be taken from us. We learned that even in the shadow of loss, there is light.

And what of the future? What do we carry with us now, all these years later? We carry the knowledge that life is fragile, that nothing is promised, that everything can change in an instant. But we also carry the understanding that within that fragility lies strength. We know now that our greatest achievements are not the tallest buildings or the grandest monuments, but the connections we forge with one another. We know that resilience is not about bouncing back to what was, but about moving forward with what remains.

In the years since, we have rebuilt the skyline, but more importantly, we have rebuilt our hearts. We have learned to live with the absence, to honor the memories of those we lost, while still making space for joy, for laughter, for life. We have learned to balance grief with gratitude, loss with love. The future is not a place free from pain, but it is a place where we can choose how we respond to it. We look forward, not with fear, but with hope. Hope that we will continue to grow, continue to learn, continue to rebuild—both the visible and the invisible, the structures we live in and the lives we lead.

The lesson is clear: we cannot erase the past, but we can shape the future. And as we move forward, we do so with the knowledge that even in the darkest moments, there is light to be found. In the cracks left by tragedy, there is room for something new to bloom. We learned this from September 11: that though the world may break, we do not have to break with it. We can rise from the ashes, stronger, wiser, and more compassionate than before. We can carry the memory of what was lost without being defined by it. We can build a future that honors the past while making room for what is to come.

So, we stand here, in the shadow of that day, not as victims of fate, but as survivors of history. We stand here with our scars, our stories, and our strength. And we look forward—with hope, with resilience, and with the quiet, enduring belief that no matter what may come, we will rise. We will rebuild. We will endure. Because that is what we have learned: that even in the face of unimaginable loss, life continues, and so do we.

Echoes in the City

In streets where silence hums an ancient song,
Echoes of a terror, timeless, blend,
Their whispers weave a tapestry so long,
A spectral waltz where shadowed memories mend.
The towers' ghosts, now fading in twilight's mist,
Resonate in dawn's fractured embrace,
Their remnants cast in hues of loss and twist,
A city scarred but braving space with grace.
Footsteps echo, tremors in stones unfold,
A world transformed, each shard a tale unspun,
A symphony where past and present hold,
In every shadow, the future's subtly run.
In every echo, through the city's breath,
A haunting dance entwines with life and death.

Notes on Echoes in the City

"Echoes in the City" delves into the emotional landscape of a city grappling with the aftermath of the September 11 attacks. The poem paints a vivid picture of a metropolis forever altered by disaster. The imagery of "silence humming an ancient song" suggests a pervasive sense of loss and mourning that fills the void left by the collapse of the Twin Towers. This silence is not merely the absence of noise but a profound, almost spiritual echo of the past, resonating through the city's streets.

The "spectral waltz" represents the interplay between memory and the present, where the shadows of the past continue to influence and shape the city's identity. The poem captures the psychological disorientation that follows such a traumatic event, where familiar spaces become haunted by the memory of what once was. The "fractured embrace" of dawn symbolizes the initial stages of healing, where the city's attempt to recover is marked by an ongoing sense of fragmentation and loss.

By reflecting on the city's transformation, the poem explores the broader theme of how places carry the weight of history and trauma. The "tremors in stones" suggest that the city's very foundation has been shaken, not only physically but also emotionally and culturally. The poem's closing lines, which describe the future subtly running through every shadow, underscore the ongoing process of healing and adaptation, highlighting the city's resilience as it navigates the new reality shaped by the attacks.

Voices of the Lost

In twilight's veil, where echoes softly spin,
The voices of the lost like whispers soar,
Their stories drift through dusk's unyielding skin,
Each tale a flicker on the cosmic floor.
Their dreams, like stardust on a midnight stream,
On spectral winds, their echoes merge with grace,
Yet linger as a hymn within our dream,
Their warmth a beacon in the darkened space.
Each name, a star in heavens' vast expanse,
Guides through storms where shadows twist and turn,
Their lives, a melody of timeless dance,
In memory's embrace, eternally burn.
In every loss, their echoes find their place,
A testament to love's enduring grace.

Notes on Voices of the Lost

"Voices of the Lost" poignantly addresses the personal and collective grief for those who perished on September 11. The poem evokes a powerful image of lost voices drifting through twilight, suggesting that while the individuals are gone, their presence continues to resonate. The "whispers" and "flickers" symbolize the fragile and elusive nature of memory, where the essence of each person is preserved in the collective consciousness.

The metaphor of dreams as "stardust on a midnight stream" conveys the idea that the lives lost have been transformed into something eternal and ethereal. This imagery reflects a philosophical view of death as a transition rather than an end, with the departed continuing to influence and guide from beyond. The poem's exploration of names as stars in the heavens reinforces the notion of immortality and the enduring impact of each individual life.

By focusing on the emotional and spiritual dimensions of loss, the poem offers solace through the belief that the voices of the deceased persist in a form that transcends physical absence. It emphasizes the importance of memory in the healing process and the idea that love and connection survive even after death.

The Sky's Silent Witness

The sky, a canvas torn by fire and flight,
Held silent witness to the towers' grief,
As crumbling pyres erased the day and night,
A tapestry where fractured memories brief.
It watched with vacant eyes as days were spun,
In shades of smoke and sorrow, chaos traced,
The sky, a witness to the storm begun,
Held secrets in its depths, by time embraced.
Yet with each dawn, the sky unveils its hue,
A canvas washed in shades of hopeful new,
It bears the scars but offers soft renew,
Where pain and healing in the twilight brew.
In every sunrise, in each whispered breath,
The sky remains a witness to the depth.

Notes on The Sky's Silent Witness

"The Sky's Silent Witness" examines the role of nature in the context of human tragedy. The sky, depicted as a "canvas torn by fire and flight," serves as a metaphor for the dramatic and destructive force of the attacks. The sky's silence suggests a cosmic indifference to human suffering, yet it also embodies a form of passive witness to the events that unfolded.

The poem explores the philosophical idea of nature as both an observer and a participant in human events. While the sky may appear indifferent, its presence as a witness implies a deeper connection to the human experience. The "fractured memories" and "chaos traced" represent the way the attacks disrupted the natural order, leaving behind a scar that is both physical and psychological.

The poem's emphasis on the sky's changing hues and the "soft renew" of dawn reflects the process of recovery and the possibility of renewal. Despite the initial devastation, there is a sense of hope and continuity as the sky gradually shifts from a symbol of chaos to one of healing. This transition underscores the idea that, even in the face of profound loss, there is potential for recovery and transformation.

The Resilience of Humanity

In trials deep, where human spirits rise,
A fortress stands from ashes cold and bare,
From shattered dreams, new hands emerge to prize,
A testament to hearts both brave and fair.
With acts of kindness woven through the storm,
The world reveals its strength amid the fray,
In every gesture, new forms start to warm,
A symphony of care that lights the way.
From chaos' roar, the silent heroes gleam,
Their courage shapes the fabric of our fate,
A tapestry where hope and hearts redeem,
And in their unity, the world finds state.
In every struggle, through the darkest plight,
The human will shines with an endless light.

Notes on The Resilience of Humanity

"The Resilience of Humanity" celebrates the capacity for human strength and solidarity in the wake of disaster. The poem portrays the emergence of a "fortress" from "ashes cold and bare," symbolizing the rebuilding and recovery process. This imagery highlights the theme of resilience, where individuals and communities rise above adversity to forge a new path forward.

The poem's focus on "acts of kindness" and "silent heroes" underscores the idea that true heroism often manifests in everyday actions rather than grand gestures. These small, yet significant, acts of compassion and support become the foundation for healing and rebuilding. The "symphony of care" suggests that the collective effort to address the aftermath of the attacks is both harmonious and transformative.

By exploring the psychological phenomenon of post-traumatic growth, the poem reflects on how people can find new purpose and strength in the face of trauma. It celebrates the human spirit's ability to adapt and thrive despite overwhelming challenges, offering a hopeful perspective on the capacity for recovery and renewal.

The Dust Settles

When dust descends and settles on the ground,
It whispers tales of loss, of lessons steeped,
In particles, the echoes are profound,
A silence deep where once the loud had wept.
The city's breath is heavy, thick with time,
Each grain a testament to all that's gone,
In every corner, echoes softly chime,
The void where shadows of the towers shone.
Yet in this quiet, hope begins to weave,
To clear the air, to start the day anew,
As dust gives way to dawn, we start to cleave,
The past and present in a clearer view.
In settling dust, a future's hope is spun,
A chance for healing with the rising sun.

Notes on The Dust Settles

"The Dust Settles" metaphorically captures the process of coming to terms with the aftermath of the attacks. The settling dust represents the transition from immediate shock and chaos to a more reflective and contemplative state. As the dust settles, it reveals deeper truths and insights about the impact of the tragedy.

The poem explores the psychological journey from initial grief to eventual healing. The "particles" of dust symbolize the fragments of memory and experience that come together to form a clearer understanding of the events. The imagery of the "city's breath" and the "void where shadows of the towers shone" highlights the profound sense of loss and emptiness that follows such a disaster.

The poem's emphasis on hope and renewal, as the dust gives way to dawn, reflects the possibility of finding clarity and purpose in the wake of destruction. It suggests that, even amidst the remnants of tragedy, there is an opportunity for healing and rebuilding. This theme of transformation underscores the resilience and adaptability of individuals and communities as they navigate the aftermath of the attacks.

Windows of the World

Through windows cracked, the world reshapes its frame,
A lens that captures both the near and wide,
In shattered glass, the past and present name,
A fractured mirror where our truths collide.
Each pane a portal to a fractured light,
A glimpse of sorrow, hope, and dreams we chase,
The glass, though broken, lets the world ignite,
The shards reflect a sky of vast embrace.
In every window's frame, a tale unfolds,
Of lives that shift, of moments caught in flame,
A world transformed, though edges may seem bold,
Through fractured views, we find our new acclaim.
In every window, truth and dreams are spun,
A vision shared, both broken and begun.

Notes on Windows of the World

"Windows of the World" uses the metaphor of cracked windows to explore the altered perception of reality following the September 11 attacks. The shattered glass represents the fragmented and disrupted view of the world that results from such a traumatic event. This imagery conveys the idea that the attacks have fundamentally changed how people see and experience their surroundings.

The poem reflects on the psychological impact of trauma, where the familiar becomes unfamiliar and new perspectives emerge. The "fractured light" and "glimpse of sorrow, hope, and dreams" symbolize the complex and multifaceted nature of the post-attack experience. The broken panes of glass suggest that while the world may appear fragmented, there is also a chance for new insights and understandings to emerge.

By examining how the attacks reshape our worldview, the poem highlights the philosophical notion that major events can profoundly alter our sense of reality. The exploration of these new perspectives underscores the resilience and adaptability required to navigate a changed world, offering both a critique and an affirmation of the human capacity for growth and renewal.

The Unseen Heroes

Beyond the headlines, where the stories blur,
The quiet heroes toil with hidden grace,
Their names remain, yet virtues never stir,
They mend the world's most fragile, darkened space.
In shadows where the crisis calls their name,
They labor with a heart both fierce and warm,
Their sacrifices form a silent flame,
Their love, a shield that weathers every storm.
Each gesture small, a monument in time,
A testament to deeds that rarely show,
Yet in their quiet acts, the truth will chime,
A chorus of the care that they bestow.
In every unseen hero's gentle hand,
A beacon of the hope they understand.

Notes on The Unseen Heroes

"The Unseen Heroes" pays tribute to the individuals who performed acts of bravery and selflessness during and after the September 11 attacks, often without recognition. The poem focuses on the quiet, often overlooked contributions of these heroes, capturing their inner strength and commitment.

The imagery of "hidden grace" and "silent flame" conveys the idea that true heroism often lies in the small, everyday actions that may not make headlines but have a profound impact. The "fragile, darkened space" represents the challenging and often unnoticed work of those who support others in times of crisis. The poem highlights the psychological and emotional aspects of heroism, emphasizing the internal motivations and moral courage that drive these individuals.

By celebrating the "unseen heroes," the poem acknowledges the importance of recognizing and valuing acts of compassion and bravery that might otherwise go unnoticed. It underscores the idea that heroism is not always about grand gestures but often about the quiet, steadfast dedication to helping others in their time of need.

What the Firefighter Saw

A tower of smoke,
spitting black,
cracking the sky open
like a wound
too wide to close.
His boots hit
the cracked pavement—
soundless in the chaos.
Sirens scream,
but the air is full of silence.
Then—
a flash.
Fire explodes,
scattering shards of lives
he never knew.
He feels the heat,
smells the burning metal,
the smell of ash,
of a city dying
beneath his feet.
He climbs,
each stair a question
he can't answer,
but each breath
takes him closer

to a decision
he doesn't know he'll make.
And then—
a crack,
a thunderous scream,
the tower leans,
buckles,
like a body in agony
before it falls.
He holds his ground.
For a second,
the world stops.
Then it crashes—
raining concrete,
dust,
bodies,
a thousand souls,
all tangled in a web
of what was
and will never be.
He runs—
into the fire,
into the smoke,
into the heart of it all,
knowing
he will never be the same.
But not yet broken.

Notes on What the Firefighter Saw

This poem, "What the Firefighter Saw," encapsulates the emotional intensity and harrowing reality of a firefighter's experience during the September 11 attacks on the Twin Towers. It employs a "concrete" style, using fragmented, visceral imagery to convey the chaos, confusion, and overwhelming sense of duty felt by first responders in the face of disaster.

The poem opens with a stark description of the sky as a "tower of smoke," immediately establishing the apocalyptic atmosphere of the day. The imagery of "cracking the sky open" and the "soundless" chaos reflects the disorienting silence amidst the catastrophic noise, heightening the sense of fear and uncertainty. As the firefighter ascends the towers, each "stair a question he can't answer," we feel his internal struggle, the futility of understanding in the face of an event that defies comprehension.

The moment when the tower "leans" and "buckles" before it collapses symbolizes the inevitable destruction, a moment of both physical and emotional breakdown. The final image of the firefighter "running—into the fire" is one of determined heroism, illustrating his resilience despite knowing he may never be the same after witnessing such profound loss.

Ultimately, the poem reflects both the personal and collective trauma of 9/11 while honoring the unyielding courage of those who risked their lives.

Down the Stairs

Each step a beat,
a pounding heart,
the walls close in—
heavy with smoke,
with the scent of fear.
Hands grasp the rail,
slick with sweat,
the world is slipping,
but I hold on tight—
keep moving,
keep going.
The air burns,
lungs scream for breath,
but there's no time
to listen.
I can't stop.
Was it a scream I heard?
Or was it my own pulse
echoing in my head?
The stairwell is empty,
but I feel them—
everyone who's left behind.
Each footfall brings me closer
to the ground,
but also farther

from something I can't name,
something lost
that I can't reclaim.
The stairwell is endless,
a loop of fear and resolve.
How long before it collapses?
How long before I break?
The weight of the building
presses down,
but my legs move faster,
my mind whispers—
survive.
What if I never reach the bottom?
What if there is no escape,
only this descent,
this fall into the unknown?
I run.
I don't know why,
but I run.

Notes on Down the Stairs

"Down the Stairs" captures the internal struggle of someone trying to escape the burning towers on September 11, focusing on the raw emotional turmoil and physical exhaustion of the descent. The poem explores themes of survival, fear, and the human instinct to keep moving even when faced with overwhelming danger. The repetitive, almost mechanical rhythm of the speaker's footsteps mirrors the sense of urgency and panic they feel as they rush down the stairs, trying to escape an impending disaster.

The opening lines introduce a chaotic, suffocating atmosphere: "heavy with smoke, with the scent of fear." The use of sensory imagery—sweat, smoke, the burning air—immerses the reader in the immediacy of the

experience. The speaker's body seems to be fighting against both physical and emotional forces, but the relentless pace of the descent represents the deep instinct for survival: "keep moving, keep going."
The repeated question of whether escape is possible ("What if I never reach the bottom? What if there is no escape?") reflects the uncertainty and helplessness that accompany a catastrophic event. The speaker grapples with the idea that, even though they are moving toward safety, they may not truly be escaping the larger trauma of the moment. Ultimately, the poem portrays not just the physical act of running but the psychological toll of trying to survive in the face of an unfathomable crisis.

In the Waiting Room

I know you're there.
Somewhere, inside that steel beast,
where fire bites the sky.
Where smoke clouds the air
and nothing is safe.
I feel you.
Not here, not beside me,
but in the space between my breaths,
in the silence I'm trying to fill
with hope,
with prayer.
I imagine you—
are you running?
Are you holding your breath,
waiting for it to end,
waiting for the sound of salvation
or the crush of the fall?
I heard the sirens.
I heard the crash,
but I didn't hear your voice—
not yet, not once.
I wonder if you're thinking of me—
or if you're thinking of nothing,
just the air,
the fire,

the weight of the sky.
Are you still climbing,
still fighting your way down
as the world above you breaks apart?
The clock ticks—
seconds,
minutes,
an hour—
but it feels like days.
It feels like lifetimes
in this room
with its sterile walls
and its cold, empty chairs.
I should be calm,
but the air feels too thick,
the walls too close,
the silence too loud.
I need you.
I need you to answer,
to call,
to say something—
anything—
to remind me
that you're still there.
I watch the news,
but all I see is the burning.
All I hear is the siren.
You're in there,
but I'm here,
stuck between the unknown
and the impossible,
waiting for a phone call

that never comes.
The hours stretch,
and I can't move,
can't breathe,
can't escape this ache.
Are you okay?
Are you scared?
Are you—?
I close my eyes
and hold my breath,
praying for a miracle
that doesn't come.
And then,
I wait for the knock.

Notes on In the Waiting Room

"In the Waiting Room" explores the emotional devastation of a wife who knows her husband is trapped in one of the Twin Towers during the September 11 attacks. The poem conveys her overwhelming sense of helplessness and the anxiety of waiting for news she dreads but desperately needs. The repeated refrain "I know you're there" establishes an immediate connection between the speaker and her husband, creating a tense, intimate atmosphere where she is both physically distant from him and emotionally tethered to his fate.

The poem's structure mirrors the cyclical nature of her thoughts: "seconds, minutes, an hour," reflecting the unbearable passage of time as she waits for any sign of her husband's survival. The sensory details—"the air too thick," "the silence too loud"—heighten her growing sense of claustrophobia and isolation. She is trapped in the "sterile walls" of a waiting room, unable to act, her body caught between dread and hope.

The wife's internal dialogue, questioning if her husband is "still climbing" or "fighting his way down," suggests that she is trying to hold onto some form of control, imagining his movements in the chaotic, burning building. Her emotional turmoil crescendos as the poem ends with an unanswered prayer, a painful metaphor for the uncertainty of that day, and the agonizing wait for news that might never come.

In My Heart, You Stay

I see you,
high above me,
where the world is burning—
where the sky is cracked,
where the air is too thick to breathe.
Mom,
are you still there?
Are you standing tall,
or are you trying to hide from the flames
like I used to hide from the thunder
underneath the covers?
I wish I could climb up
and hold your hand,
whisper in your ear
that I'll be okay.
But I can't.
I can only sit here
and wait
and imagine your face
like it's a picture I can't touch.
Did you think of me
when it all began?
Did you think of my hands,
my smile,
my voice calling your name

before everything shattered?
I wonder if you're scared.
I wonder if you're praying
for a way out,
for the sound of a door
that will open,
that will bring you home.
I wish I could hold you,
even though you're far away.
Even though I can't reach you,
I feel you.
I feel you
in every breath I take.
And though the world is dark,
I will keep you in the light.
In my heart,
you stay.
I won't forget.

Notes on In My Heart, You Stay

"In My Heart, You Stay" captures the profound emotional turmoil of a young daughter who is separated from her mother, trapped in the Twin Towers on September 11. The poem conveys the child's deep sense of longing, fear, and helplessness, as she is forced to confront the horror of not knowing whether her mother will make it out alive. The daughter imagines her mother "high above me," emphasizing the physical and emotional distance between them. The repetition of "I can't" highlights the child's frustration and inability to act, symbolizing the helplessness felt by many in the face of the catastrophe.

The poem uses tender imagery to illustrate the child's yearning for reassurance, asking if her mother thought of her in the moments before disaster struck: "Did you think of me / when it all began?" This evokes a sense of vulnerability and a desire for connection in the face of overwhelming uncertainty. The reference to seeking comfort, like hiding from thunder under the covers, shows the child's instinct to seek safety and reassurance, a contrast to the inescapable danger her mother faces.

Despite the uncertainty, the daughter finds solace in her unbreakable emotional bond with her mother, promising, "I will keep you in the light. / In my heart, you stay." This closing sentiment is both a tribute to the enduring connection between them and a powerful expression of love amid the tragedy.

Looking at the Ashes

I stand where silence used to roar,
where lives once danced on floors of glass,
and now—
nothing but rubble,
smoke,
and the ghost of a skyline.
The air still tastes like fire.
The ground is scarred,
a scar I never thought I'd see—
deep, jagged,
like the hole inside me
that won't heal.
I remember the sound
before the world collapsed—
the snap of glass,
the howl of metal,
the scream of a thousand hearts
frozen in time.
How did we survive?
What magic saved me
while the sky turned black
and the towers fell like broken dreams?
I can still hear the voices—
those who didn't make it,
the ones who walked away

into the night,
never to return.
We were here,
and now we're gone,
and I am left to carry
the weight of what was
and what never will be again.
The smoke rises—
curling like memories,
like a past that refuses to die,
and I try to breathe,
try to see
the world beyond the ash.
But all I know is this—
I walked through the fire,
and now the world will never be the same.
And neither will I.

Notes on Looking at the Ashes

"Looking at the Ashes" captures the emotional aftermath of a survivor witnessing the devastation of the 9/11 attacks. The speaker reflects on the destruction around them, grappling with the profound sense of loss and trauma while also questioning how they managed to survive when so many did not. The poem opens with a stark image of what remains—rubble and smoke, remnants of a once-thriving place now reduced to "ghosts" and "scarred" land. The juxtaposition of these physical images with the emotional weight of survival creates a disorienting sense of grief, as the survivor is forced to reconcile their presence amid the destruction.

The line "How did we survive?" serves as a poignant moment of introspection, signaling the survivor's confusion and guilt over their fate. The poem evokes both personal and collective trauma, especially through the repeated mentions of those who perished—"the ones who walked away / into the night, never to return." The speaker reflects on the emotional and psychological cost of surviving a catastrophe where the world, as they once knew it, has been irreparably altered.

In the final stanzas, the speaker acknowledges the permanent impact of the event. The line "I walked through the fire, / and now the world will never be the same. / And neither will I" underscores the enduring transformation wrought by such a devastating experience—both personally and collectively. The survivor is left to face a world that will forever bear the marks of that day.

From the Sky

I hover above the shattered world,
a bird with no wings,
chasing stories in the smoke.
Below, the towers burn,
like giants falling into the sea—
silent,
save for the roar that never ends.
The city stretches,
fractured beneath my gaze,
streets that once pulsed with life
now lost in ash,
beneath the weight of the sky.
I can't tell where the buildings end
and the smoke begins.
Everything is swallowed,
dissolved into a haze
that smells like fire and fear.
I lean forward,
trying to capture the moment—
trying to make sense of this disaster
that defies every word
I've ever written.
There are no words for this.
Only images that burn into your mind,
frozen in time,

the planes
the flames
the fall.
I can't look away.
The city is a wound,
bleeding into the sky.
I think of the people,
the lives crushed in a second,
families waiting,
phones unanswered.
I think of the stories untold—
the voices lost in the dark.
And still, I write,
scribbling frantic notes,
even as the world crumbles beneath us.
The helicopter sways,
but I stay focused,
watching,
recording,
holding the truth in my hands.
What else can I do?
I turn away from the wreckage,
but it follows me,
chasing me,
like a shadow that will never leave.

Notes on From the Sky

"From the Sky" immerses the reader in the harrowing perspective of a news journalist flying over New York City in a helicopter on September 11, 2001, as the attacks unfold. The poem begins with the journalist observing the towering infernos below, where the "giants [are] falling into the sea," immediately invoking the vast scale of the destruction.

The image of a "bird with no wings" emphasizes the journalist's detachment—an observer, yet powerless, watching the calamity from above, as the world collapses below.

The poem conveys the surreal experience of trying to report on an event so immense that words seem inadequate. "There are no words for this" captures the dissonance between the overwhelming visual reality of the disaster and the limitations of language. The journalist is caught between a need to document history and the emotional weight of the devastation, which no article or headline could fully encapsulate.

The recurring imagery of "fire," "fall," and "the city is a wound" underscores the unrelenting violence of the day. The final lines, where the journalist records the events while feeling personally overwhelmed, reflect the emotional toll on those tasked with witnessing and relaying history. The poem captures the struggle between the duty to report and the haunting knowledge that the tragedy is inescapable, following the journalist long after the story has been told.

How Do You Prepare?

How do you prepare
for the day the world cracks?
When the ground beneath your feet turns brittle,
and the sky—once your constant—
becomes something you can't trust?
Do you steel yourself against the storm,
train your mind like a soldier,
shut down your heart
so it doesn't break when the bodies fall?
Do you memorize the sounds of sirens,
the ones that wail like a prayer unanswered,
so you can learn not to flinch?
Is there a way to hold your breath
without suffocating on the smoke of tomorrow?
You can't prepare for this,
not in any way that makes sense.
You can count the hours,
but time doesn't warn you when the bombs will fall.
You can practice breathing under pressure,
but you won't know what it's like
until the air turns thick with terror,
until the sky falls down in pieces.
Do you prepare by imagining
that your family, your friends,
are somewhere safe,

somewhere far from the violence?
Can you imagine,
when your body trembles with the fear
that they might be right there—
trapped in the smoke,
lost in the crowd?
Do you prepare by asking God,
by asking fate,
to keep the worst from happening?
To send you signs,
to show you a path,
when the world tilts,
when the ground shakes
and your city becomes a battlefield?
You could try to prepare with knowledge—
watch the footage of the past,
read the stories of those who lived through wars,
learn the history of humanity's failures.
But nothing will teach you
how to be ready
for a nightmare unfolding in real-time.
Do you prepare by training your eyes,
to look for signs of danger
before it's too late?
By learning to read the tension in a room,
the way people's shoulders stiffen,
the way their hands tremble when they think no one is looking?
By learning to recognize the lies
we tell ourselves to survive?
Or do you prepare by thinking of love,
by holding on to the things that keep you human—
the warm embrace of a child,

the laughter of a friend,
the soft hum of music in the distance?
Because in the end,
those are the things that might save you—
the memories,
the heartbeat of hope
that refuses to die.
But still, when the plane's engines roar,
when the earth cracks wide open
and the sound of destruction rises up like a flood,
you will realize—
you were never ready.
You never could have been.
No one ever is.
All you can do
is hold on.
You will either be broken,
or you will break open.
You will either fight,
or you will fall.
But one thing you will not do—
is stand still.
The moment will arrive,
and the world will change,
and in that split second
you will learn the only truth:
survival is not in the preparation,
it's in the will to face what you cannot know.
How do you prepare?
You don't.
You can only endure.
You can only survive

by holding on to what remains
of who you were,
and letting the rest slip away.
Because, in the end,
what is left after the storm
is not what you learned,
but who you became
when everything else burned.

Notes on How Do You Prepare?

The poem *"How Do You Prepare?"* explores the psychological and emotional struggle of preparing for an unimaginable event—specifically, a catastrophic tragedy like the 9/11 attacks. The speaker grapples with the limitations of human preparedness when confronted with an event so overwhelming that it shatters normalcy and throws the world into chaos. The poem asks, *"How do you prepare for the day the world cracks?"* which sets the tone for the central dilemma: no matter how much we try to prepare mentally for a disaster, the reality of facing one is far beyond our control or comprehension.

From the outset, the speaker acknowledges that traditional forms of preparation—emotional or mental fortitude, strategic planning, or even imagining the worst—are insufficient. The poem's repeated questioning and the imagery of "steel[ing] yourself" and "shut[ting] down your heart" reflect the emotional toll such events can take. The speaker suggests that although one can try to ready themselves for tragedy, nothing can truly equip them for the sheer scale of chaos that unfolds.

The poem also highlights the dissonance between trying to prepare and the unavoidable emotional impact of catastrophe. The speaker explores the futility of intellectual readiness, illustrating that there are no instructions for how to survive a disaster of such magnitude. The lines *"no one ever is"* express this stark realization.

In the final stanzas, the poem turns toward resilience. The speaker contemplates human connection—love, memories, and relationships—as potential sources of strength. Ultimately, the poem asserts that true survival lies not in preparation but in the ability to endure. The closing lines, *"what is left after the storm / is not what you learned, / but who you became / when everything else burned,"* emphasize that after the devastation, it is not the lessons or knowledge that remain, but the transformation of the person who has weathered the storm. This reflects the core message: survival is not about preparation, but about the will to adapt and become stronger through unimaginable suffering.

The Weight of Memory

I carry it like a stone
in the pocket of my chest,
heavy and cold,
its edges worn smooth
by the passage of years.
Sometimes, I forget it's there—
it sinks into the folds of my mind,
quiet as a shadow,
slipping beneath the surface
of daily life.
But then, a sound,
a smell,
a flicker of light,
and it rises,
sharp and sudden,
like a breath I can't catch.
It is a whisper of voices long gone,
a flicker of faces that once smiled
now trapped in the glass of old photographs.
I hold them,
pressed against my ribs,
like fragile wings in a jar—
so close,
and yet always just out of reach.
There are days I wish I could shake it off,

this weight that presses me to the earth.
But when I try,
it clings tighter,
refusing to be forgotten,
demanding to be remembered.
It is the warmth of your hand in mine,
the sound of your laugh echoing
in the hallways of my mind.
It is the softness of your voice
calling my name in the dark,
a sound that haunts me
long after silence takes its place.
Memory is a song that never ends,
a melody that loops in the quiet of the night,
pulling me back to places
I thought I had left behind.
It drifts like smoke,
settling in the corners of my thoughts,
always there,
always just out of reach.
I have tried to put it down,
to lay it at the foot of time,
hoping it would stay,
but it follows me—
like the stars that trail behind
as the earth spins,
untouched,
unfathomable.
Sometimes, I dream of forgetting,
of clearing my mind,
of waking one day and finding
that the weight is gone—

but that is a lie I tell myself.
For even in the stillness,
even in the light of day,
it pulls at my soul,
and I am bound to it,
forever tethered to the past.
There is no escaping it—
not really.
No matter how far I run,
no matter how many years I add to my life,
it is there,
this weight of memory,
woven into the fabric of who I am,
woven into the very air I breathe.
It has shaped me,
made me soft in places I cannot name,
strong in places I never knew were weak.
It is the echo of love that once was,
the mark of loss that never heals.
And yet, I would not cast it away.
For though it presses like a stone,
it also grounds me,
anchors me in a world
that often seems to float away.
Without it, I would be lost,
untethered,
adrift in a sea of faces
that never belonged to me.
So I carry it,
this weight of memory,
like a secret folded in the palm of my hand,
like the last letter you wrote,

the one I never sent.
It is a part of me now—
as much as breath,
as much as blood—
a burden and a blessing,
woven together,
inextricable,
forever with me,
forever mine.

Notes on The Weight of Memory

"The Weight of Memory" explores the emotional burden and complexity of memory, focusing on how it shapes our identity and experience. The poem is about the persistent nature of memory, how it can be both a source of comfort and a weight that we cannot escape. The speaker likens memory to a stone in the chest, something heavy and constant, at times forgotten but always present, waiting to resurface with sensory triggers—a sound, a smell, or a fleeting moment that brings the past crashing back.

The poem's imagery—such as memories "pressed against [the speaker's] ribs" like fragile wings or the haunting "song that never ends"—illustrates the way memories stay with us, never truly fading, no matter how hard we try to leave them behind. The weight of memory can feel like a burden, but it also anchors us, grounding us in the reality of who we are. It shapes our emotional landscape, affecting how we love, how we grieve, and how we carry forward the marks of our past.

In the end, the speaker acknowledges that memory is inescapable and entwines itself with the very fabric of our lives. The poem reflects both the painful and profound nature of memory, a gift and a curse that defines our existence.

Hope in the Darkest Times

In the darkest times,
when the world feels broken,
and shadows stretch long,
it's easy to forget
that light once lived here.
But still,
in the hollow spaces between breaths,
there is a flicker.
It's a whisper at first,
a soft murmur that says,
"Hold on."
A fragile thread spun from something
greater than despair,
something that refuses to break.
It hides in the quiet moments,
in the curve of a smile,
in the warmth of hands held close.
It doesn't shout;
it doesn't demand attention.
It waits patiently,
like the first star in the sky
after the sun has dipped.
When the night feels endless,
and the weight of the world crushes the chest,
hope is the spark you can't quite see

but can feel in your bones.
It is the quiet courage
that keeps the heart beating,
even when the world has fallen silent.
Hope doesn't wear a crown.
It doesn't need to be seen.
It lives in the resilience of the human spirit,
in the courage to wake each morning
when the darkness threatens to swallow everything whole.
There is strength in the smallest acts:
the turning of a page,
the opening of a door,
the reaching of a hand.
Each of these is a defiance,
a rebellion against the void,
a whisper back to the night
that says, "I will not be consumed."
Even in the deepest sorrow,
hope wears no face,
but it can be heard
in the breath of a mother
soothing her child in the dark.
It is found in the letter from a friend,
the unexpected kindness of a stranger,
the shared laughter of those who refuse
to let the weight of the world
pull them under.
Hope is the quiet hum in the silence,
the heartbeat of a world that won't let go.
When all feels lost,
hope is the thread we follow,
however faint it may seem.

It may not bring answers,
but it brings strength,
and that is often enough.
Hope is not a grand gesture,
not the bursting of flames,
but the steady glow of a candle,
held through the storm.
And when the darkest times have passed,
and the light begins to return,
we will look back
and know that it was hope
that guided us through the night.
Hope, ever steady,
ever present,
never truly gone—
just waiting for us
to believe in it again.

Notes on Hope in the Darkest Times

"Hope in the Darkest Times" is a poem that explores the quiet yet resilient power of hope during moments of intense hardship and despair. It acknowledges how darkness—whether personal or collective—can feel overwhelming, but it suggests that hope is never truly extinguished, even in the bleakest moments. The poem emphasizes that hope does not come with grand gestures or dramatic proclamations; instead, it is found in the small, everyday acts that keep life moving forward, even when it feels like the world is falling apart.

The speaker begins by illustrating how hope is often a "flicker" or "whisper," something subtle and easily overlooked. It is in the quiet resilience of human connection—the "smile," the "warmth of hands held close"—and in the courage to persist despite the overwhelming weight of the world. Hope is personified as something patient and persistent, akin to the “first star in the sky” or the "quiet hum in the silence," emphasizing its ability to endure even when the world seems silent or lost.

The poem concludes by affirming that hope is a thread, a guiding force that helps us move through adversity, even if we can’t see it clearly. Ultimately, hope is the quiet strength that allows us to survive dark times and emerge into light, knowing it was hope that carried us through.

The Burden of Silence, After All is Said and Done

After all the words have fallen,
like leaves to the ground,
there is only the quiet—
heavy,
dense,
and filled with echoes that never leave.
Silence comes as a shadow,
a weight that presses against the chest,
presses against the soul.
It doesn't shout.
It doesn't demand.
It simply *is*,
a presence,
a void.
And in that void,
all the things we didn't say
linger like smoke,
clinging to the air
long after the fire has died.
We spoke of love,
but not enough to heal the cracks.
We spoke of pain,
but never enough to face it.
We danced around the truth,

circled it like a question we were too afraid to ask.
And now—
now we are left with this silence,
a chasm between us,
bigger than any word could fill.
It is in the spaces between breaths,
the pauses that come when no one dares to speak.
It's the coldness in the room,
where warmth once lived.
The silence settles in corners,
and it waits—
waits for us to acknowledge it,
to confess what we left unsaid.
There were words—
so many words—
but they were hollow,
echoes of things we thought we wanted
but never truly meant.
And now we're stuck in the quiet,
the silence that swallows all of them,
leaving us adrift
with only the weight of what's missing.
We thought silence was the absence of noise,
but it is so much more—
it is the absence of connection,
the absence of truth.
It is the space where love should have been,
where understanding should have thrived,
but where only distance grew instead.
Now, after everything has been said,
after all the promises and good intentions,
the silence settles in like dust.

It coats the edges of our lives,
and we breathe it in,
unwilling,
unwitting.
And yet, there it is—
sitting beside us,
between us,
beneath us,
always there,
as if it has always been.
What do we do with this burden?
This weight of silence that presses down,
weighing heavy on our hearts,
on our tongues,
on our thoughts?
Can we speak into it?
Can we shatter it with the truth we left unspoken?
Or does silence only grow in the presence of regret?
We said we were fine—
but fine was never enough.
We said we were strong—
but strength without understanding is hollow.
We said we were happy—
but happiness can't live in the spaces
where silence reigns.
It is a quiet ache,
a persistent hum in the background,
like a song you can't quite remember,
but know is always there,
distant and yet familiar.
The burden of silence is not something we can see,
but we feel it,

always,
lingering in the air,
clinging to the walls.
After all the words have fallen,
after all the chances to speak have passed,
we are left to face what we avoided—
the truth we buried beneath layers of silence,
layers of *not enough*.
We cannot outrun it.
We cannot speak it away.
It stays,
a part of us,
woven into the fabric of our lives,
woven into the spaces between our thoughts.
The burden of silence is not just the things we didn't say,
but the things we didn't ask,
the things we didn't hear,
the things we couldn't forgive.
And now, after all is said and done,
it sits there,
silent and unyielding,
a weight we must learn to carry.
And still—
still—
we hope that somewhere,
beneath this silence,
a new voice will rise.
That the silence will give way,
eventually,
to words that are true,
to words that heal,
to words that break the quiet

and bring us back to each other.

Notes on The Burden of Silence

"The Burden of Silence" poignantly reflects the emotional aftermath of a traumatic event, drawing on themes of unspoken pain, unresolved grief, and the haunting presence of silence that follows great loss. Though the poem is not explicitly about September 11, its exploration of the heavy weight of silence can be interpreted as directly linked to the emotional and psychological toll of that day and its aftermath.

On September 11, 2001, the world was thrust into chaos and horror, and in the immediate aftermath, there were no adequate words to describe the magnitude of the loss, the confusion, or the grief. In the poem, the speaker reflects on the silence that follows the unspoken words, the things left unsaid, which mirrors the collective sense of helplessness and emotional paralysis many experienced in the wake of the attacks. The "burden of silence" becomes a metaphor for the overwhelming and inescapable grief that followed the destruction, as people struggled to express the enormity of their sorrow and fear.

The poem speaks to the disconnect between what people try to say ("we thought silence was the absence of noise") and the truth they are unable or unwilling to face. In the context of September 11, this can reflect the difficulty in articulating the impact of the event—whether personal or societal—where words seemed insufficient to convey the scale of loss. The silence was not just a lack of sound, but a deeper absence of connection, of healing, and of understanding. It symbolizes the emotional void left by lives lost, unspoken prayers, and the collective mourning that seemed too vast to articulate.

Ultimately, *"The Burden of Silence"* mirrors how trauma, especially from an event as catastrophic as September 11, leaves people with a silent weight that can't be immediately expressed or shared, and may take years to begin to process.

A New Normal

In every street where footsteps mark the shift,
A new routine emerges from the fray,
Old ways dissolve, and boundaries gently lift,
As life adjusts to what has come to stay.
The rhythms change with grace, a subtle shift,
A new lens through which the world now appears,
Security and care in every rift,
And fears that linger softly disappear.
Yet through the change, a strength begins to form,
A resilience built from lessons learned anew,
A world adjusted, as the sky transforms,
A future shaped by all we strive to view.
In every new normal, hope is sown,
A testament to seeds we've gently grown.

Notes on A New Normal

"A New Normal" explores the process of adjusting to a changed reality following the September 11 attacks. The poem reflects on how daily routines and societal norms shift in response to trauma, capturing the psychological adaptation required to embrace a new way of life.

The imagery of "footsteps mark the shift" and "boundaries gently lift" symbolizes the gradual process of adapting to a new reality. The poem explores how old ways dissolve and new routines emerge, highlighting the resilience and flexibility needed to navigate change. The "subtle shift" in rhythms suggests that while the changes may be incremental, they are nonetheless significant and transformative.

By focusing on the concept of a "new normal," the poem addresses the philosophical idea of finding stability and meaning in a world that has been irrevocably altered. It reflects on the human capacity to adjust and find hope in the face of ongoing challenges, emphasizing the potential for growth and renewal even in the aftermath of tragedy.

Epilogue: Rising from the Ashes

In the silent echoes of a city's mournful sigh,
Where shadows of the past stretch long and wide,
We gather fragments of our shattered sky,
And piece together hopes from deep inside.
From the ashes of the towers' final fall,
Where dust and memory interlace with grief,
We find within our hearts a fervent call,
To build anew from sorrow's raw relief.
In every crack of glass and faded light,
A future's whisper stirs the dawn's embrace,
And through the veils of night and endless fight,
We glimpse the promise of a brighter place.
As names etched in the stars guide us through pain,
And unseen heroes rise from darkened seams,
We learn that in the loss, new strength is gained,
And from the ruins, we create our dreams.
For though the world has changed in ways profound,
And echoes of the past may never cease,
In every corner, hope and love are found,
And in our hearts, we forge a lasting peace.
So let the story of our scars remind,
That from the deepest wounds, new light will grow,
And through the darkness, strength of heart we'll find,
As from the ashes, vibrant futures show.
In every sunrise, every whispered prayer,

We build the world anew with care and grace,
And in the journey from despair to where
We find our place, and cherish love's embrace.
September 11, 2024

About Alex Telman

Alex Telman is a globally recognized spiritual healer, author, and one of the country's most read poets. With over 45 years of experience, he has dedicated his life to helping individuals break free from negative energies, trauma, and spiritual blockages. His transformative work has empowered a diverse range of clients, including celebrities, business leaders, educators, and everyday individuals, guiding them toward emotional well-being, personal growth, and spiritual fulfillment.

From an early age, Alex demonstrated extraordinary abilities to perceive and remove harmful energies and entities, a gift that first emerged when he was just three years old. This rare talent led him to study with psychic masters across the globe—Afghanistan, France, Sweden, Israel, England, and Australia—each recognizing his unique gifts and helping him refine his craft.

In addition to his healing practice, Alex has practiced as a barrister, teacher, university lecturer, and small business owner, offering a well-rounded perspective on healing that combines spirituality with practical action. He is also an accomplished author, whose writings inspire and uplift readers by exploring the depths of human emotion and the power of self-healing.

Through his sessions, Alex has helped countless individuals overcome emotional turmoil and reclaim their lives. His work transcends cultural and geographical boundaries, offering profound healing to those in need. His mission is simple yet powerful: to guide people back to their authentic selves, helping them live with purpose, peace, and fulfillment.

With a career built on compassion, wisdom, and deep spiritual insight, Alex remains a beacon of hope for anyone seeking to overcome their struggles and wanting to step into a life of clarity and joy.

Acknowledgement for cover art: pixabay

Other Titles by Alex Telman

Non Fiction

Think Like a Modern Guru

Mastering Hypnosis: Complete Step-by-Step Manual, Case Studies, and Sample Scripts

From Cursed to Cured: 100 True Stories of Healing from Curses

Connecting to the Afterlife: a how-to guide

Your Journey from Death to Rebirth

Empower Your Sundays: Unlocking Inner Strength for a Resilient Life

The Truth Behind the Creation Story: A Journey Through Reincarnation

Practical Mentalism in a Nutshell

Reprogram Your Mind in a Nutshell

Meditation in a Nutshell

Alex Telman in Quotes

Novels

A Happy Death

One Life, Half Lived

Down and Out in Byron Bay

God Speaks: A Journey Through Creation in His Own Words

Jesus Speaks: The Man Behind the Miracle in His Own Words

Poetry

Telman: The Complete Haiku 1974-2024

Homeless in New York

ALEX TELMAN

Burning Echoes of Time
From Dawn to Dusk: the life cycle in sonnets
Eternal Echoes: The Tapestry of Time and the Unseen
Snapshots of People I Have Never Met
Legends and Lessons: 36 Myths Unveiled
A Measure of Time: The Eternal Voyage of Self
Ashes of Verses: Poems Burned But Not Forgotten
Reflections on Solitude: A Poetic Journey Through The Lonely Mind
Your Friendship is a Museum
Whispers to Bella

Don't miss out!

Visit the website below and you can sign up to receive emails whenever Alex Telman publishes a new book. There's no charge and no obligation.

https://books2read.com/r/B-A-YBSCC-VVLZE

BOOKS 2 READ

Connecting independent readers to independent writers.

Did you love *Echoes of September 11*? Then you should read *Down and Out in Byron Bay*[1] by Alex Telman!

[2]

Dear Reader,

As you embark on this journey through the pages of "Down and Out in Byron Bay," I invite you to immerse yourself in the raw, emotional landscape of a place that has profoundly shaped my identity. These stories are not just recollections of my life; they are an homage to the vibrant tapestry of Byron Bay—its beauty, its struggles, and the intricate dance of change that defines it.

In a world that often rushes forward, I find solace in reflecting on the past, seeking to understand how it informs our present. The tales shared within these pages weave together personal experiences with the larger narrative of a town that has transformed from a haven for

---

1. https://books2read.com/u/3JqnNv

2. https://books2read.com/u/3JqnNv

free spirits into a bustling tourist destination. As I recount my own evolution amid the backdrop of Byron's shifting identity, I hope to capture the essence of resilience that resides within us all.

This book is also a call to recognize the power of storytelling. Each narrative is a thread in a greater tapestry, illustrating the interconnectedness of our lives and experiences. It is in sharing these stories that we honor the past and inspire future generations to cherish their own journeys.

I write not just for myself, but for the countless souls who have walked these streets, shared laughter and tears, and forged connections that transcend time. As you read, I encourage you to reflect on your own stories, the places that have shaped you, and the memories that linger like the scent of salt in the air.

Thank you for joining me in this exploration of identity, community, and the beauty found in both the chaos and the calm. Together, may we celebrate the complexities of life and the indomitable spirit of a place that continues to evolve.

*

In the sun-soaked paradise of Byron Bay, Finn Sullivan's life unfolds amidst the vibrant chaos of art, love, and longing. Through a tapestry of poignant reflections and raw emotion, Finn grapples with the weight of expectations, the struggle for connection, and the relentless pursuit of his dreams.

What happens when ambition and isolation collide?

After a serendipitous meeting with Finn's parents in 1974, the author forged a lifelong friendship with the Sullivan family. As Finn grows, so does the complexity of his journey—a journey marked by moments of joy and heartache, artistic ambition, and the yearning for deeper connections.

When the author receives a box filled with Finn's undated writings, he embarks on a quest to piece together the story of a young man navigating the tumultuous waters of adulthood. These writings reveal not only Finn's struggles but also the universal themes of love, loss, and the search for belonging.

Join Finn as he confronts his past, embraces the power of vulnerability, and discovers the transformative magic of human connection.

This collection invites you to reflect on your own journey and the threads that weave us all together. Discover the beauty of resilience and the hope that blossoms in the face of uncertainty.

Will Finn find his way back to the life he longs for?

A poignant exploration of the human experience, Finn's story resonates with anyone who has ever dared to dream, faltered in the pursuit, and sought to rise again.

Read more at www.AlexTelman.com.

www.ingramcontent.com/pod-product-compliance
Lightning Source LLC
LaVergne TN
LVHW050559160826
845677LV00011B/2378

* 9 7 9 8 2 3 0 6 7 4 2 9 0 *